Why Do Dogs Have Wet Noses?

To my grandchildren,
Shani, Ravi, Chevi, Dassi, Cora, Mateo,
Santiago and Centainne —SC

Why Do Dogs Have Wet Noses?

By Stanley Coren

Kids Can Press

First paperback edition 2008

Text © 2006 Stanley Coren

This edition is only available for distribution through the school market by Scholastic Book Clubs.

ISBN 978-1-55453-756-3

CM PA 10 0 9 8 7 6 5 4 3 2 1

Kids Can Press acknowledges the financial support of the Government of Ontario, through the Ontario Media Development Corporation's Ontario Book Initiative; the Ontario Arts Council; the Canada Council for the Arts; and the Government of Canada, through the BPIDP, for our publishing activity.

Published in Canada by
Kids Can Press Ltd.
25 Dockside Drive
Toronto, ON M5A 0B5

Published in the U.S. by
Kids Can Press Ltd.
2250 Military Road
Tonawanda, NY 14150

www.kidscanpress.com

Edited by Shana Hayes and Charis Wahl
Designed by Marie Bartholomew
Illustrations by Céleste Gagnon

Photo Credits

Every reasonable effort has been made to trace ownership of, and give accurate credit to, copyrighted material. Information that would enable the publisher to correct any discrepancies in future editions would be appreciated.

Abbreviations: t = top; b = bottom

Cover photograph: Photodisc, Inc.

p. 11: Dale C. Spartas/Corbis; p. 13 (t): photos.com; p. 25(b): Melissa McClellan; p. 28: Dale C. Spartas/Corbis; p. 30: Shaun Best/Reuters/Corbis; p. 34 (t): Robert Llewellyn/Corbis; p. 35: Tom Stewart/Corbis; p. 45: Dick Hemingway; p. 46 (t): Index Stock, (b) Tim Davis/Corbis; p. 47 (t): Ivy Images; p. 51: Photodisc/Getty Images; p. 54: Dale C. Spartas/Corbis; p. 55: Keven R. Morris/Corbis; p. 57: Dale C. Spartas/Corbis; p. 63: Ivy Images.

All other photos Photodisc, Inc., Stockybyte, JUPITERIMAGES.

The hardcover edition of this book is smyth sewn casebound.
The paperback edition of this book is limp sewn with a drawn-on cover.
Manufactured in Buji, Shenzhen, China, in 12/2010 by WKT Company

CM 06 0 9 8 7 6 5 4
CM PA 08 0 9 8 7 6 5 4 3 2 1

Library and Archives Canada Cataloguing in Publication

Coren, Stanley
   Why do dogs have wet noses? / by Stanley Coren.

ISBN 978-1-55337-657-6 (bound). ISBN 978-1-55337-658-3 (pbk.)

1. Dogs—Miscellanea—Juvenile literature. I. Title.

SF426.5.C69 2006   j636.7   C2005-902156-X

Kids Can Press is a ʃ◉ℾℐ∫™ Entertainment company

Contents

Chapter 1

How Humans and Dogs Became Friends

Dogs are full of secrets. They have their own mysterious way of thinking. They use their own language when they talk to other dogs and to people. (Dogs understand other dogs; humans often don't have a clue about what dogs are saying.) Dogs' eyes, ears and noses give them a picture of the world that's very different from humans'. When dogs are born they already know how to do some things and to act in certain ways. How do they know this? And how did dogs and people come to love each other in the first place?

Let's see if we can solve some of these mysteries together.

Are dogs just tame wolves?

Some dogs look a lot like wolves.
Others, like Saint Bernards and
dachshunds, don't look like wolves at
all. So did dogs really start out as wolves?
How can we tell?

One way is by their ability to make families.
If, say, a wolf father and a dog mother can
make puppies together, and their puppies can
have puppies, then the wolf and dog are the
same kind of animal (or *species*).

Dogs can have puppies with wolves all right,
but also with jackals, coyotes, dingoes, African
wild dogs and even some kinds of foxes. So
dogs are probably a mixture of all these animals.

That's why there are so many
different-looking dogs.

8

The tail tells the tale

Huskies, the sled dogs of the North, look almost exactly like arctic wolves. How do you know which you're looking at? Wolves never have their tails high and curled over their backs. Wolf tails always droop downward.

Did people tame dogs or did dogs tame dogs?

Some say the first dog was a wolf cub that a prehistoric man tamed and kept as a pet. Others believe that dogs tamed themselves!

Prehistoric men were good hunters but messy housekeepers. After they killed and ate animals, they tossed the bones and scraps in heaps near the edge of their village. Some wolves got an idea: "With all those good bones and stuff lying around, why bother hunting?" Instead, they stayed around the village. The villagers were happy that the wolves ate the garbage — that kept down the smell and the bugs. And there was a bonus: the wolves barked when a dangerous animal or a stranger came close, so the village was safer. Since the friendliest animals were allowed right into the village and got the best food and care, some dogs probably decided that it was better to be tame. The people just rewarded them for being tame and good dogs instead of wild animals.

Well, some did. Neanderthal cavemen never made friends with dogs. When the Ice Age arrived and food became scarce, Neanderthals did not have dogs to help them find and capture food. This is one reason why the Neanderthals disappeared and the dog-loving Cro-Magnon cavemen survived to become us — modern humans.

Isn't that a really good payback for the bits of food, shelter and love that we gave to dogs?

How long have dogs and humans been friends?

Dog bones and dog fossils from about 14 000 years ago were found with human bones and human fossils. What does this mean? Dogs have lived with people for a long time. Cats have lived with people for only 7000 years.

The smallest dog in history

What's the smallest dog ever? A Chihuahua? No, a Yorkshire terrier owned by Arthur Marples of Blackburn, England. It was just $2^1/_2$ inches (6 cm) tall measured at the shoulder and only $3^3/_4$ inches (9.5 cm) from its nose to the start of its tail. About the same size as a one-pound block of butter, but it weighed a lot less — only about 4 ounces (113 grams), the same as a quarter-pound hamburger without the bun!

The biggest dog in the world

Zorba, an English mastiff, is the biggest dog ever recorded. He weighed 343 pounds (156 kg) and measured 8 feet 3 inches (252 cm) from his nose to the start of his tail.

Can a dog be too small for its own good?

To stop the pooping pigeons in New York City's Bryant Park, specially trained hawks were let loose. The hawks would also spot and kill rats. One hawk named Galan spied a tiny furry thing in the bushes. He swooped down to catch it. Unfortunately, he had someone's Chihuahua in his claws. Oops!

The fastest animal in the world?

Everyone knows the cheetah is the fastest animal in the world. Cheetahs can run 65 mph (105 km/h), but only for short runs that might last a few seconds. Greyhounds can run at their top speed for distances of as much as 7 miles (11 km). The average dog can run about 19 mph (30 km/h), and greyhounds can run at speeds of 30 to 35 mph (48 to 56 km/h). So the cheetah would win the short sprint, but in any distance race the greyhound would leave the cheetah panting in the dust.

The slowest dog?

No one has measured which breed is the slowest, but dogs with short legs and heavy bodies can't get up very much speed. The three contenders for dog most likely to finish the race last? The English bulldog, the dachshund and the basset hound.

Some dogs seem slow, although they can be fast when they want to be. One of these is the big Newfoundland, who would rather lie around and sleep than run. Back when a fire in the hearth was the main source of heat for the home, Newfoundlands would lie in front of the fireplace for hours without moving. Because they looked just like big fur rugs, they became known as "mat dogs."

How many dogs are there?

Add the total number of people in the United States, Canada, Great Britain and France. Got it? That's how many dogs there are in the world. The best guess is over 400 million dogs.

It's hard to find out the exact number of dogs because some dogs roam the streets and nobody really owns them.

Are there more wolves than dogs?

There are a lot fewer wolves than dogs. If you add together all the wolves from all the countries around the world, you'd have about 400 thousand wolves. And there are 400 million dogs. That means there are a thousand times more dogs in the world than wolves!

Why are there so many dogs?

When she is 5 to 18 months old, a female dog can have her first litter of puppies. Puppies take 58 to 70 days to be born. A mother dog can have two litters of puppies each year. Each litter has between 6 and 10 puppies. About half of the puppies will be girls, and in 5 to 18 months, they will start having puppies. Of course, these female puppies will also have puppies. And so on. One female dog and her female children could produce 4372 puppies in seven years!

How many dog breeds are there?

Do you like tiny, energetic dogs? Or are big, slobbery dogs your favorite? Each breed of dog has its own size, shape, color and personality. You can pick a dog that is exactly right for you. There are over 700 different breeds of dogs, although some are very rare. Special organizations, called kennel clubs, keep records on different breeds. Most kennel clubs allow only a few of these many breeds to be registered. The American Kennel Club accepts about 150 different breeds, and the Canadian Kennel Club accepts about 160 breeds of dogs.

Which are the most popular breeds of dogs?

Each country and every period in history has had its favorite kind of dog. Over the past few years in the United States the five most popular breeds of dogs have been the Labrador retriever, the golden retriever, the German shepherd, the dachshund and the beagle. In Canada the top five are the Labrador retriever, the golden retriever, the German shepherd, the poodle and the Shetland sheepdog. The favorites in Britain are the Labrador retriever, the German shepherd, the golden retriever, the West Highland white terrier and the cocker spaniel. Notice that the top three dog breeds are the same for all three countries. Out of all the breeds of dog in all the countries, the most popular is the Labrador retriever — and it's been that way for quite a while now.

Which are the national favorites?

CANADA	UNITED STATES	GREAT BRITAIN
☆ Labrador retriever	☆ Labrador retriever	☆ Labrador retriever
☆ Golden retriever	☆ Golden retriever	☆ German shepherd
☆ German shepherd	☆ German shepherd	☆ Golden retriever
☆ Poodle	☆ Dachshund	☆ West Highland terrier
☆ Shetland sheepdog	☆ Beagle	☆ Cocker spaniel

Unpopular dogs?

Some dog breeds stop being popular, and if enough people aren't interested in breeding them these types of dogs may disappear completely. That is why you will never see a Spanish pointer, a turnspit dog or a long-haired greyhound, because they are extinct. In 2002, only 17 otterhounds and 23 harriers were registered with the American Kennel Club, so these dog breeds may be in danger of disappearing next.

What is the most ancient breed of dog?

Paintings and carvings of greyhounds and salukis have been found in Egypt that are more than 3000 years old. Those early images of greyhounds and salukis look almost the same as the two breeds look today. Even their names suggest they're special. *Greyhound* comes from a mistake in translating the early German name *Greishund*, which means "old" or "ancient" dog. Also greyhounds aren't usually gray. *Saluki* is Arabic for "noble one."

18

How old is your dog?

You may have heard that one year in a dog's life is equal to seven years in a person's life. That's not really true. Puppies grow and change very quickly. By their first birthday, dogs have all the physical abilities that a 16-year-old human has. When they are two years old, dogs are a lot like 24-year-old humans. After two years, each year adds about five human years to a dog's age.

Want to figure out your dog's age in human years? Let's say your dog is 12 years old. Start with 24 years for her first two years, then add 5 years for each of her next 10 years. She is 74 years in human years (24+50). The average age that people live to is 74 years, and 12 years is the average life span for dogs.

The oldest dog who ever lived

The oldest dog on record was an Australian cattle dog named Bluey. He died when he was 29 years and 5 months old. In people years he was more than 160 years old!

Do different dog breeds live longer or shorter lives?

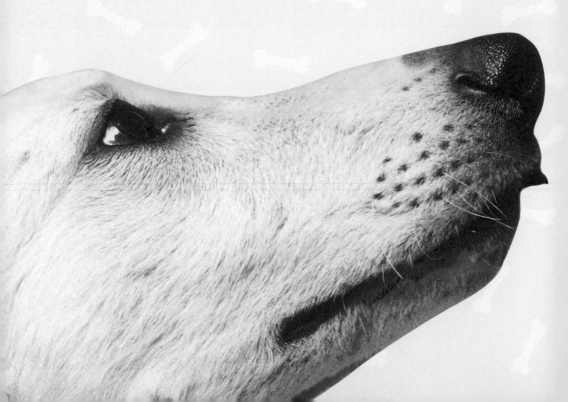

Small dogs live longer than big dogs. For example, the Irish wolfhound is the tallest breed of dog, and they usually live 7 years. The Great Dane has an average life span of 8 years. Standard poodles live about 11 years, while miniature poodles live about 13 years. The small, tough Jack Russell terrier and the tiny Chihuahua both live to about 14 years.

Facing the facts

The shape of your dog's face can also tell how long he will live. Dogs with sharp, pointed faces that look like wolves usually live longer. Dogs with very flat faces, like bulldogs, often have shorter lives. Of course, dogs that are well cared for can live a lot longer than average.

Chapter 2

How Dogs See the World

Different eyes, ears and noses are specially designed to help animals find good food and stay alive. Rabbits stay alive by running away from things that want to eat them, so rabbits have eyes that see in almost every direction — even what's happening behind them! That's why it's so difficult to sneak up on a rabbit. Monkeys have eyes that see into the distance really well. If they didn't, they would miss the branches they try to reach when they swing through the trees. The first dogs were hunters, and all dogs have eyes, ears and noses designed to help them do that job.

The eyes of a night hunter

Dogs see best at night or in dim light. The hunters that dogs descended from hunted in the dim light of early morning or late evening, so they needed to see well in this type of light to find their prey. Long thin cells in your eye (called rods) let you see when things are pretty dark. Dogs have more of these rods than people do. They also have a special mirror-like surface, called the tapetum, in the back of their eyes. When you shine a flashlight into a dog's face at night, his eyes seem to glow in a bright greenish, weird way — that's the tapetum. It bounces light back, giving the rods more of a chance to see things.

Do dogs appreciate rainbows?

Dogs can see color but not as well as people can. Short, fat cells in the eye (called cones) see color. Dogs have fewer cones than people, which makes dogs a bit colorblind. They can tell the difference between blues and yellows, but they can't see the difference between reds and greens. It is even difficult to train a dog to use the blues and yellows that she can see. It seems that dogs just don't pay much attention to color.

The wrong toy?

A lot of popular dog toys are red or orange, not because dogs like that color but because those colors are very bright and easily seen by the human who is buying the toy. However, if you throw a red toy onto the grass and your dog runs right past it, he is not being stubborn or dumb. For a dog's eye, the red of the toy and the green of the grass are the same color, except that the red is just a bit darker.

If it moves, I'll catch it!

A hunter doesn't have to see small details, like letters printed on a page, but moving things might be something to chase and eat. Even though dogs can't see small things as well as humans can, they see things that move much better than we do. A person standing absolutely still 300 yards (275 meters) away is almost invisible to a dog. But a dog can easily see a person standing a mile (1.5 km) away waving his arms!

I'm listening

Which shape of
ear hears better,
pointed or floppy?
Dogs with pointed
ears hear better than dogs with floppy ears. The
floppy part of the ear covers the hole that the
sound has to enter, and this prevents some of it
from ever getting in. Dogs with pointed ears
can turn them to catch more of the sound
coming from a particular direction. People can't
hear as well as dogs can. Sounds that may not
bother us, such as the sound of a vacuum
cleaner, may be painfully loud to a dog.

I hear you, Squeaky

Not only do dogs have better hearing than
people, but dogs can hear a wider range of
sound. Dogs are more likely to hear high-pitched
sounds, like squeaks, than humans are. Some
hunters and police officers use the "silent" dog
whistle to tell dogs what to
do. It isn't really silent — the
sound it makes is at a pitch
that dogs can hear but is too
high for people to hear.

I can't hear you at all

Loud noises can damage a person's hearing, which is why people often use ear protectors in noisy places. Dogs can also be hurt by loud sounds. Hunting dogs, like retrievers, often are near very loud noises from rifles and shotguns when they are used for hunting. This is one reason why many hunting dogs become deaf at a young age.

Is that an earthquake I hear?

Humans can't hear subsonic sounds (very low rumbling sounds), but some dogs can. Dogs with big square heads and large ears, like the Saint Bernard, are the best at hearing these low sounds. Subsonic sounds make it through the snow and help the Saint Bernard find and rescue people trapped in avalanches. Before an earthquake, subsonic sounds are made when rocks move and break deep in the earth. In China and other places around the world, scientists use the special hearing abilities of dogs to predict earthquakes far enough in advance to save human lives.

The nose knows

If dogs could talk, instead of saying "seeing is believing" they would probably say "smelling is believing." A dog is about a thousand times more sensitive to smells than a person.

   Deep inside a dog's nose are several yellowish folded layers with cells that pick up tiny droplets carrying smells through the air. You have the same folds, and if we unfolded those layers in your nose, they would be about the size of four postage stamps. In dogs, they would unfold to the size of a large bandanna. Humans have 5 million smell-detecting cells, and dogs can have more than 220 million. Even though their brains are smaller than ours, the part of the brain that figures out smell is four times larger in dogs than it is in people.

It's a stinky job, but somebody has to do it!

Humans put dogs' sense of smell to work. You probably already know that dogs have been used to detect people carrying guns, bombs, drugs and even food they are trying to smuggle into countries. But did you know they can sniff out where rats are hiding, where dead bodies are (even underwater) and can even tell where termites are hiding in the walls of houses? Police use dogs' sense of smell not only to track runaway criminals but also to detect arson — when someone has deliberately set a building on fire.

Engineers working on a pipeline carrying natural gas suspected that some gas was leaking, but their best scientific instruments couldn't find out where. Leaked gas can cause explosions or fires, so specially trained dogs were called in. The dogs found nearly 150 dangerous gas leaks — even though the leaks were often buried 40 feet (12 m) underground!

Doctor dog?

Dogs are being trained to use their sense of smell to find cancers that may be too small to be spotted by doctors. They can even find lung cancer by sniffing a person's breath!

Why do dogs have cold, wet noses?

There are two reasons dogs have cold, wet noses. One is to help keep them cool. When water evaporates, the place that it left gets cooler. Lick the end of one of your fingers, then wave your hand in the air. You will notice that the wet finger feels cool as the water leaves it. When a dog gets hot, he pants so water evaporates from his mouth and his wet nose to keep him cool.

The other reason for a wet nose is that wet things pick up small objects well. Just as a wet cloth picks up dust better than a dry one, a wet nose collects more of the tiny droplets of good-smelling chemicals from the air — and dogs love to check out different smells.

 ## I recognize that nose

The pattern of markings on each dog's nose is as unique as the pattern of lines that make up your fingerprints. A dog's nose print is often used to identify her in the same way we use fingerprints to identify people. Ask your mom or dad to help you get a copy of your dog's nose print. First dab some food coloring (never use ink) on her nose, then carefully press a notepad against it. You may have to try a couple of times to get a clear, unsmudged print, but when you do, you will see the pattern that belongs to only your dog.

Why dogs don't go to cooking school

Dogs are very sensitive to bitter tastes and hate them. They also avoid certain sour tastes like lemons or grapefruits. An interesting fact is that dogs like sweet tastes a lot more than cats do. This is probably because dogs can survive by eating only fruit for quite a while. Cats, on the other hand, are pure meat eaters (with a side of milk and cheese). No self-respecting cat would ever eat fruit — even if his life depended on it!

Dogs don't pay as much attention to taste as people do. Our sense of taste comes from special cells inside the taste buds on the tongue. Dogs have about 1700 taste buds, and people have around 9000. Dogs can taste sweet, sour, salty and bitter the same way people do, but they also have some special taste buds that are tuned to meaty and fatty tastes. This makes sense since they came from wild hunters and meat eaters.

Strange doggy snacks

Taste may not be particularly important to dogs because they have an instinct to gulp down their food. Left over from their hunting days, the instinct to eat quickly developed in dogs so that they had their food safely in their bellies before some bigger animal came along to steal it. However, this way of eating can sometimes lead to interesting menu choices.

Dierdre McLennan in Cornwall, England, has a beagle named Zach. Since she's had him, Zach has eaten a ring, two cell phones, a check for £10 000 (about $20 000), slippers, shoes, 14 cushions and numerous pairs of socks and pants. Mrs. McLennan complained that "he is six years old now and should have more sense." Perhaps the sense Zach needs is a better sense of taste!

A homemade dog treat

Want a safe and easy treat to give your dog? Make up some chicken bouillon (you can use powder or bouillon cubes). Pour it into an ice cube tray and freeze it. Now you have an inexpensive and safe dog treat. If people ask you what you are giving your dog, you can tell them "pupsicles."

Some dangerous tastes

Be careful what you give your dog as a treat. You may love chocolate, macadamia nuts, grapes and raisins, but these can all kill your dog. Onions, even when they are cooked, are also bad. Anything with caffeine, such as coffee, tea or certain flavors of soda pop, like colas, can be harmful, too. Some people give their dogs apple or pear cores, or maybe peach or pear pits with some of the fruit still on them. Unfortunately apple and pear seeds as well as plum, peach and apricot pits contain arsenic, which can be deadly to your pet — and you, too!

Chapter 3

How Dogs Talk

A folk tale from Zimbabwe explains that dogs know how to speak — but have decided not to. According to the story, the hero, Nkhango, made a deal with the dog Rukuba. If Rukuba stole some fire from one of the gods, people would be dog's friend forever. The dog kept his part of the bargain and gave people fire. Later Nkhango asked the dog to help him hunt dangerous animals, stand guard, herd animals and do other difficult jobs. Finally Nkhango decided that Rukuba should be a messenger. This was just too much. After all, dog had given people fire and he felt he should be allowed to just lie near it and keep warm and cozy. Rukuba thought, "People will always be sending me here and there on errands because I am smart and can speak. But if I can't speak, then I can't be a messenger." From that day, dogs have chosen not to speak. But dogs do speak — if you can understand them.

Why do dogs bark?

How do you feel when a dog is barking at you? Are you ever afraid that the dog is angry and is making threats? Sometimes that may be true. But most often, even though the noise is loud and scary, barking is really a message for the dog's family. Barking is a kind of alarm that tells the family, "Something is happening here! You should check this out!" This type of barking is usually two or three barks, then a space, then another two or three barks and so on. It would sound like "woof, woof, woof ... woof, woof ... woof, woof, woof ..."

How do you get your dog to stop barking?

When their dog starts to bark, a lot of people yell at the dog to try to make the barking stop. They shout, "Be quiet! Stop that noise!" But that's the wrong thing to do. What the dog hears is "woof, woof … woof, woof, woof …" Sound familiar? To the dog, shouting sounds the same as the alarm the dog is already barking. So the dog thinks, "I barked, and now my family is starting to bark, too, so I must be doing the right thing." This just makes the dog bark louder!

To get your dog to stop barking, just remember that she wants you to check to make sure everything is okay. Walk up to your dog. Look in the direction she is barking. Tell her everything is safe in a nice voice and give her a pat. She will usually think, "My family listened and nothing is wrong, so I can stop barking."

Why do dogs howl?

Dogs do a lot of barking and wolves do a lot of howling. But the opposite isn't true. Dogs don't howl a lot and wolves don't bark a lot. When wolves howl they're saying, "I am here. Come and join me." Howling wolves attract other members of the pack who then join in and howl along. Dogs howl to say the same thing wolves do, but a dog usually howls only when locked outside or feeling lonely. The polite way to answer a howling dog is to howl back. But what would the neighbors say? I don't suggest you try it! A better idea is to bring your dog inside to keep you company. The howling will stop when he's no longer lonely.

Why do some people believe that if a dog howls someone will die?

Have you ever heard that a howling dog means someone will die? Superstitions like this are part of every culture and often have a logical explanation. This superstition probably began when someone in a house was very sick. The family likely kept their dog outside or locked up so it wouldn't bother anyone. Because the dog was alone and lonely, it would start to howl. If the sick person died, the family remembered the howling and thought, "Our dog howled the night Grandfather died. Maybe he was howling because he knew Grandfather was very sick and would die." The next time a member of that family heard a dog howl they might have said, "The dog is telling us that someone else is going to die." Other people heard this and became afraid when they heard the howling — all because of a lonely dog!

Give Squeaky a kiss

Dogs tell us they are angry by making low-pitched sounds like growls and grumbles. When they are trying to tell us they need love and help, dogs make high-pitched sounds like whines and whimpers. Try this. Give the back of your hand a big, noisy, squeaky kiss. When your dog hears that high-pitched sound, she will look at you carefully and may come close to make sure you are all right. She may give you a little lick — if she feels you need some love and comfort.

The language of the tail

How can you tell if a dog is happy? When he's wagging his tail? That's partially true. How fast the dog wags his tail tells you how excited he is. How high the tail is tells you a lot, too. If the tail is high and the wags are small but fast, the dog might be feeling annoyed or could be saying, "I'm boss around here." If the tail is lower than usual and the wags are slow, it could mean "I'm worried" or "I don't understand what you want." When the tail is halfway between high and low and the wags are very big swings it means "I'm happy and I know you will take care of me!"

The language of the ears

Ever send a message with your hands? Dogs can send messages with ear signals. Ear language follows some of the same up-and-down rules as tail language. If the ears are up high and lean to the front, the dog is either angry or is feeling bossy. If the ears are low and pulled back, the dog is worried or scared. You have to look carefully to see these signals in floppy-eared dogs.

Worried or scared
floppy-eared dog

Worried or scared
pointed-eared dog

Angry or bossy
floppy-eared dog

Angry or bossy
pointed-eared dog

Do you want to play?

Dogs love to play. When they're ready to romp, dogs put their front legs flat on the ground to the elbows so their rear ends are up and their tails are wagging. This is called a "play bow." They may give a little play bark, which sounds like "harrr-ruff!" If you get down on all fours and slap the ground with your forearms flat to the elbow, your dog might take that as an invitation to play. He may answer by giving his own play bow, or he may just dash around or maybe jump on you to start a wrestling match.

Stinky ink

What's so interesting about the tree, the fence and the fire hydrant? When your dog sniffs somewhere other dogs have visited, she is reading a big doggy newspaper and learning the latest gossip about her dog neighbors. Dogs write messages to other dogs in urine. Different smells in a dog's urine can tell other dogs whether the dog leaving the message is female or male, old or young, sick or healthy, happy or angry.

Why do male dogs raise their legs to pee?

One message that dogs read from the local lamppost is the size of the dog that left that message. By raising their legs, male dogs aim higher on the tree or lamppost and make themselves seem larger. Some wild dogs in Africa even try to run up tree trunks while they are urinating to appear to be very, very large.

Urine messages can be more of a problem than just being smelly. In Croatia, lampposts began to fall down. Scientists discovered this was because a chemical in the urine of male dogs was rotting the metal!

Why do dogs roll in garbage?

Rotten eggs, smelly garbage and poo — yum! These may be the best smells in the world — to a dog. Rolling in smelly stuff is an instinct dogs inherited from their wild hunter ancestors. A strong smell hides the dog's own smell, making it easier to sneak up on other animals. Hunters that don't smell like hunters catch more prey.

Why do dogs hate cats?

Dogs and cats use body signals to talk. Both use the same signals, but with different meanings. A dog sees a cat swooshing his tail in a big, swinging motion and bounces over to say hello, expecting a happy greeting. What happens? He gets scratched and bitten. Why? When a dog wags his tail with a big, swinging motion it's a friendly signal. A cat wags his tail this way when he's angry. This dog thinks the cat is a liar and will never trust another cat. The good news — dogs can learn to understand the cats they live with. Other cats, however, are still liars and enemies!

Can dogs love cats?

One cold day in Bristol, England, a
gang of mean boys stole a kitten. They threw it into a pond
and waited for it to drown. Suddenly, a Labrador retriever
named Puma dashed into the pond and grabbed the kitten.
Puma must have thought this was an accident because he
brought the kitten out of the water and laid him at the boys'
feet. The boys laughed and threw the kitten back into the
water. Puma leaped into the water again, but this time he swam
to the other side of the pond with the kitten and ran home
with him. When his family opened the door, he rushed past
them and laid the kitten down next to the heat vent and then
stood guard over him to make sure that no one would hurt him
again. The family kept the kitten and named him Lucky
because he was so lucky to find a friend like Puma.

Can a dog learn to be a cat?

A man in Philadelphia brought home a young
puppy named Flash. His cat, Mildred, had just had
a litter of kittens and adopted Flash, treating him
just like one of her kittens. Flash began to act just
like a cat. His favorite toys became cat toys. He
even learned cat manners, including the special
cat habit of washing his paws with his tongue,
then using them to clean his face and ears.

Chapter 4

How Dogs Think

Dogs can do many things that humans can't. Some dogs are faster than people. We're certain that dogs can smell and hear better than people. For their size, dogs are very strong. But people are smarter than dogs. However, we have to be extra smart if we want to understand what a dog is thinking.

How do dogs think?

Dogs think, learn, solve problems and have feelings. The way a dog's brain is set up is similar to our brain. If you want to compare their thinking to people's, dogs are about as smart as a two- or three-year-old child. This means dogs can learn to understand about 150 to 200 words, including signals and hand movements with the same meanings as words.

Smarter than you think

Sometimes dogs learn to do things that people have never taught them. Saint Bernards patrol mountain paths in the Alps after snowstorms to find lost travelers. The dogs work best in teams of three or more. If they find someone in trouble, two dogs lie down beside the person to keep him warm. One of these will lick the person's face to try to wake him up. Meanwhile, the third dog will go back to find rescuers and guide them to the scene. These dogs are never given any special training. Young dogs learn the job just by joining the older ones on patrols and watching them do their work.

Not smart enough to drive

Johnny Vaughan, host of a British television show, watched his sports car crash because of his bulldog, Harvey. Returning from a trip to the veterinarian, Johnny stopped to let Harvey have a little exercise. When Johnny stepped out of the car, Harvey jumped across the seat and knocked the gearshift into drive. Then Harvey jumped off the seat and hit the gas pedal, which made the car race into the rear end of a van with a loud crunch. When Vaughan called the insurance company, however, they said that they wouldn't pay for the expensive repairs to the car because he had let someone drive who didn't have a valid driver's license!

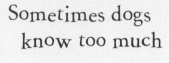

Sometimes dogs know too much

A burglar broke into a home in Dewsbury, England, but had to make a quick escape through a window when he heard the family returning home. The burglar might have gotten away if he hadn't left his dog, Roxy, behind. The homeowners found the abandoned dog, put a leash on her and took her for a little walk. Roxy happily led the couple straight home to her master, who lived only a few city blocks away. A police search later found the evidence that convicted him of the crime. The homeowner had this to say: "He should have left the dog at home — it wasn't his best friend that night."

Can dogs do math?

Although dogs may not be able to tell you the square root of nine, they do know a little addition and subtraction. Researchers showed dogs a few dog treats, and then lowered a screen to hide the treats. Treats were added or removed, or the pile was left alone, then the screen was removed. When the number of treats had changed, the dogs stared at them for a longer time than if the pile remained the same. Dogs were more interested and took more time when there were more (or fewer) treats than they had seen earlier. This suggests that dogs have some ability to count and maybe to add and subtract. But don't give your dog a pocket calculator — he's still likely to use it as a chew toy!

Why do pointers point?

Certain hunting dogs smell an animal, look directly at its hiding place and freeze. Sometimes they stop so quickly that one of their front legs remains in midair. This position is called *pointing*. Dogs that do this best are called *pointers*, but other dogs, like *setters*, will also point. Pointing is left over from the hunting behaviors of wolves. When a wolf sees a deer, he can't bark at the other wolves to say, "Hey, there is a deer over here!" because the deer would hear it and run away. Instead the wolf stops moving and stares directly at the deer. This tells the other wolves which direction to look in and lets them quietly gather for the hunt. Human hunters make use of dogs with this instinct. Pointers and setters tell hunters where birds or rabbits might be hiding but do it silently so the animals won't be scared away.

Why do collies herd?

It would take ten men to control the same size flock of sheep that one man and one collie can. Without dogs, it would be much more expensive for humans to keep flocks of animals. Collies can keep flocks of sheep, herds of cattle and even gaggles of geese together and steer them in a particular direction. Like many dog behaviors, herding comes from the hunting instincts inherited from wolves. When wolves hunt, they circle a herd of deer or wild sheep to keep them together. Next they move the herd to a place where it will be harder for them to run away when the wolves attack. Herding dogs work very hard. One dog is doing the same job that a whole pack of wolves would do together — except herding dogs don't finish the hunt by killing and eating the herd.

What is a "collie"?

The word *collie* comes from the small black-faced sheep found in Scotland called collie sheep. Dogs that herded these sheep came to be known as collie dogs. The name stuck and is now used as part of the name of several different dog breeds — even if that dog will be used to herd cattle, pigs, goats or geese and may never see a collie sheep!

Why do puppies chew shoes?

Puppies want to explore their world. Because they don't have hands, a puppy explores with her eyes, ears, nose and mouth. Once your slipper is in her mouth, she may find it has an interesting taste. She will chew awhile to see if it might be food, and that's long enough to turn it into a mess. Another reason puppies chew is that they are growing teeth. Their gums get itchy and chewing helps. Want to stop the chewing that's caused by teething? Wet an old washcloth and put it in the freezer. Give that to the pup to chew and it will make his gums feel better. When it thaws, just wet it and freeze it again and you'll have an everlasting chew toy!

Dogs in trouble

Curiosity may have killed the cat, but dogs get into trouble, too. Curious dogs get stuck in tight places and swallow toys. German shepherds seem to be the unluckiest, or the most curious, breed. Border collies, German shorthaired pointers and Great Danes also find lots of trouble. Some dogs even manage to find trouble when someone is trying to help fix their last problem. Tinker was a German shepherd who had to be operated on by a veterinarian because he had swallowed a large toy. The operation was successful, but he had to be operated on again a few hours later. While no one was watching, Tinker ate the plastic tubes and valves the veterinarian was using to put medicine directly into his bloodstream after the operation!

Do dogs dream?

Because a dog's brain is so much like a person's, it shouldn't be a surprise to learn that dogs dream. You can tell when your dog is dreaming by watching him. When he falls into a deep sleep, he breathes in a very regular way, with his chest rising and falling in a slow rhythm. When a dream starts, your dog's breathing changes. Breaths aren't as deep and don't follow a regular rhythm. You may see odd muscle twitches, and your dog may make some sounds. Look closely at his eyes and you should see them moving behind his closed lids. His eyes are moving because your dog is looking at his dream images as if they were actually happening.

Dogs that snore

Just like people, some dogs snore. Dogs with flat faces, like pugs and bulldogs, are the most likely to snore. A Neapolitan mastiff named Sumo snored so loudly that the sound broke the local noise pollution laws. Someone even took Sumo's owner to court because people in the nearby apartments were being kept awake by the sound!

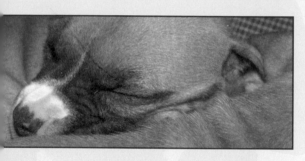

How much time do dogs spend dreaming?

Small dogs have more dreams than big dogs. A toy poodle may dream once every ten minutes, and a large mastiff or a Great Dane may dream only once an hour. Even though big dogs have fewer dreams, their dreams last longer. The amount of time that a dog spends dreaming depends on how old he is, just as it does in people. Young puppies spend more of their sleep time dreaming than adult dogs do.

What do dogs dream about?

Does your dog chase rabbits in his dreams?
How can we know what they're dreaming if
they can't tell us? There is a special part of the
brain in all animals (including humans) that
keeps us from acting out our dreams while we
are having them. When scientists stop that part
of the brain from working, animals move
around and do what they are dreaming about.
Without that part of the brain working,
dreaming border collies herd dream sheep,
sleeping hunting dogs search for dream
birds, and dreaming rottweilers
guard their homes from dream
burglars. So dogs dream about
doing doggy things.

Dreams about dogs

Some people believe our dreams *about* dogs can be used to predict the future. They believe a dream about a black or gray dog might predict bad things to come. Other common dream interpretations are that dreaming about a white dog means good things will happen, and a red-and-white dog means a sick person will get well quickly. Dreams about dalmatians, since they are both black and white, mean there will be many changes in your life or many friends and enemies. Dreams about dogs barking are good luck, while dreams with howling dogs are bad luck. Growling and biting dogs in your dreams mean that someone you know can't be trusted. Dreams about a dog licking your face are supposed to mean love and good fortune — but open your eyes first to make sure you're dreaming — it might just be your dog trying to wake you up.

The devil in disguise?

In Irvine, California, three men stole two pit bull pups from an animal shelter. Their plan was to sell the big, tough dogs to some criminals who ran an illegal dog-fighting ring. When they brought the dogs to a veterinarian for vaccination shots, the dogs were identified as Chihuahuas! Microchips in the dogs' ears also proved these were stolen dogs. The thieves now have plenty of free time — in their jail cells — to learn how to identify different dog breeds!

The sign of the dog

Each year in the 12-year-cycle Chinese calendar is identified with an animal. If you are born in a certain animal's year, "this is the animal that hides in your heart." Chinese folk tales say that Buddha called all the animals to him to say good-bye when he left the earth. Only 12 came — the rat, ox, tiger, rabbit, dragon, snake, horse, sheep, monkey, rooster, pig and, of course, the dog, so Buddha named a year after each one. People born in 1958, 1970, 1982, 1994, 2006 and 2018 are all born under the sign of the dog and are supposed to have certain dog behaviors and personalities. This makes them honest, loyal and champions of justice. They can also be stubborn, worry too much and dislike crowds or noisy parties. Based on your birthday (or your personality), are you a dog? Is someone you know a dog?